# MANCHESTER'S
# NORTHERN QUART

The greatest meer village

D1325163

720.
942
733
**TAY**

# MANCHESTER'S NORTHERN QUARTER

## The greatest meer village

Simon Taylor and Julian Holder

MANCHESTER
CITY COUNCIL

ENGLISH HERITAGE

Published by English Heritage, Kemble Drive, Swindon SN2 2GZ
www.english-heritage.org.uk
English Heritage is the Government's statutory adviser on all aspects of the historic environment.

© English Heritage 2008

Images (except as otherwise shown) © English Heritage or © Crown copyright. NMR.

First published 2008

ISBN 978 1 873592 84 7
Product code 50946

*British Library Cataloguing in Publication Data*
A CIP catalogue record for this book is available from the British Library.

Brought to publication by Joan Hodsdon, Publishing, English Heritage, Kemble Drive, Swindon SN2 2GZ

Edited by Sara Peacock.

Page layout by Swales & Willis Ltd, Exeter.

Printed in Belgium by DeckersSnoeck

Manchester City Council made a financial contribution towards the publication of this book.

Front cover
*The Wholesale Fish Market, detail.*
*[DP028891]*

Inside front cover
*Surviving pattern of fireplaces and flues from lost houses on Mangle Street.*
*[DP028478]*

Frontispiece
*Warehouse to the rear of 7 Kelvin Street.*
*[DP028470]*

Dedicated to the memory of Dr Ian H Goodall, 1948–2006

# Contents

# Acknowledgements

The production of this booklet was greatly assisted by Kate Borland, David Hilton, Warren Marshall and Matt Cawley of Manchester City Council; Henry Owen-John and Crispin Edwards of English Heritage; Marion Barter, formerly of English Heritage, now of The Architectural History Practice; the late Robina McNeil, formerly of Greater Manchester Archaeological Unit; Carol Gausden of the Manchester Early Dwellings Research Group; and the staffs of Greater Manchester County Record Office, Chetham's Library and the Local Studies Section of Manchester Central Library. Figure 14 is redrawn with the kind permission of Christopher Chalklin.

Thanks are also due to Clare Hartwell of the Buildings Books Trust (Buildings of England) who commented on the text.

We are also grateful for the assistance and support provided by our colleagues in the Research and Standards Departments of English Heritage. The photographs were taken by Keith Buck, Bob Skingle and Simon Taylor. Allan T Adams produced the drawings and maps and John Cattell, Colum Giles, Ian Goodall and Adam Menuge commented on the text. Thanks are also due to Kathryn Morrison for sharing her research on Manchester shops. The survey and research was undertaken by Allan T Adams, Naomi Archer, Keith Buck, Ian Goodall, Adam Menuge, Bob Skingle, Simon Taylor, Matthew Withey and Nicola Wray.

# Foreword

Manchester is the archetype city of the Industrial Revolution. Its city centre with the Town Hall is also acknowledged as possibly the finest Victorian commercial district in England. The city's historical legacy is both important in itself and a huge asset for today and for the future. Far from being a barrier to change and renewal, it has been successfully placed at the centre of the city's recent urban renaissance to produce highly distinctive and dynamic new environments. Stand-out successes such as the rejuvenation of Castlefield and the resurgence of the Victorian and Edwardian warehouse district, centred on Whitworth Street and Princess Street, speak volumes for the positive contribution made by the historic environment in this respect. Against this celebrated backdrop, the contrasting landscape of narrow lanes and wide boulevards in the city centre's Northern Quarter has been reborn and is now the subject of ongoing social and economic transformation.

Change has been ever present in England's towns and cities and the historic fabric of the Northern Quarter is testimony to that. The historic environment, however, is a finite resource, one that lends cherished elements of distinctiveness to our everyday urban neighbourhoods and makes a significant contribution to the quality of our lives. Because of this it is important that, while ushering in the new, the old is not overlooked or forgotten. By telling the story of the Northern Quarter through its historic buildings this book aims to demonstrate their significance and explain why they are such an asset to regeneration. Both English Heritage and Manchester City Council wish to ensure that, as prosperity returns, the Northern Quarter remains a distinctive place, wearing its layers of history with pride.

Lord Bruce-Lockhart, Chairman, English Heritage
Councillor Sir Richard Leese, Leader, Manchester City Council

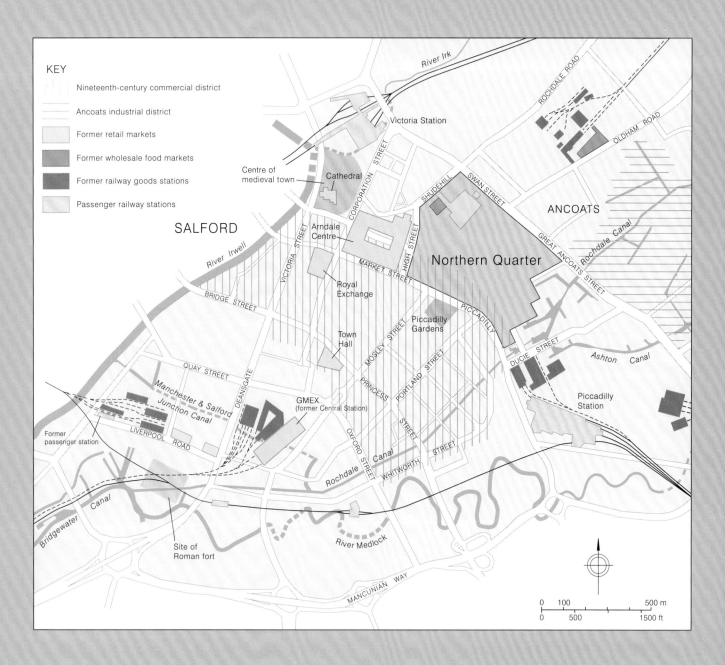

KEY

Nineteenth-century commercial district

Ancoats industrial district

Former retail markets

Former wholesale food markets

Former railway goods stations

Passenger railway stations

River Irk

Victoria Station

ROCHDALE ROAD

OLDHAM ROAD

SALFORD

Centre of
medieval town

Cathedral

CORPORATION STREET

SHUDEHILL

SWAN STREET

ANCOATS

River Irwell

Arndale
Centre

Northern Quarter

GREAT ANCOATS STREET

Rochdale Canal

BRIDGE STREET

VICTORIA STREET

Royal
Exchange

MARKET STREET

HIGH STREET

PICCADILLY

Town
Hall

MOSLEY STREET

Piccadilly
Gardens

PORTLAND STREET

DUCIE STREET

Ashton Canal

QUAY STREET

DEANSGATE

GMEX
(former Central Station)

PRINCESS STREET

STREET

Piccadilly
Station

Manchester & Salford
Junction Canal

LIVERPOOL ROAD

OXFORD STREET

Rochdale Canal

WHITWORTH STREET

Former
passenger station

Bridgewater Canal

Site of
Roman fort

River Medlock

MANCUNIAN WAY

0    100                    500 m

0        500              1500 ft

# 1

# Introduction

The Northern Quarter is a part of central Manchester which lies just over 400m to the east of the city's medieval cathedral and a mere 250m from the towering textile mills of Ancoats to the north-east. It is an area of approximately 0.3sq km and is bounded to the west by Shudehill and High Street, to the north by Swan Street, to the east by the Rochdale Canal and to the south by Piccadilly (Fig 1). It is an area that has seen over two and a half centuries of changes, which are still evident in the street patterns, in the names of the roads and, most importantly, in the juxtaposition of contrasting historic buildings. In the Northern Quarter, brick-built Georgian artisans' houses, complete with purpose-built top-floor workshops, rub shoulders with multi-storeyed steel-framed Edwardian textile warehouses, Victorian pubs, markets and commercial chambers, and 20th-century department stores. Many areas of the city centre have been remoulded by comprehensive and successful regeneration, and since the mid-1990s the Northern Quarter too has increasingly developed from an overlooked district, languishing in a state of economic inertia, to a significant element in the attraction and distinctiveness of Manchester's city centre. Both English Heritage and Manchester City Council are keen to ensure that, as the area moves into a new phase of development, the historic integrity that is so vital to its character is not lost.

Formal efforts to both protect and revitalise the Northern Quarter began back in 1987 with the designation of the Smithfield and Stevenson Square conservation areas by Manchester City Council. A regeneration study, also commissioned by the Council, followed in 1993 which resulted in the area's promotion as a focus for creative activities and indeed the adoption of the name 'Northern Quarter'. The likelihood of rapid change became evident in the 1990s, as did the fact that little was known about the architecture and topographical character of the area. English Heritage promptly undertook a comprehensive assessment of the buildings in both the Northern Quarter and neighbouring Shudehill. The assessment involved a rapid external survey of all standing structures, supplemented by documentary research, and resulted in a report in 2001 (The Shudehill and Northern Quarter of Manchester: 'An Outgrowth of Accident' and 'Built According

*Fig 1 The centre of Manchester and the location of the Northern Quarter.*

to a Plan' *Architectural Investigation* Reports and Papers B/066/2001), which forms the basis of this booklet.

Despite the refurbishment and conversion of a number of important and historic buildings in the Northern Quarter, long-term neglect of others means that there are still many individual buildings that have fallen into a serious state of disrepair. Effective remedial action will inevitably involve some loss of historic fabric while incidental damage can be catastrophic in scale (Figs 2 and 3). The aim of this booklet is not to suggest that the Northern Quarter should be preserved unchanged, but rather to draw attention to the enormous variety and particular character of what survives and raise awareness of its significance in the wider story of the city, thereby providing a basis for better decision-making.

Fig 2 *The burnt-out shell of a warehouse in Dale Street. The scaffolding had been erected for the refurbishment that was underway in May 2007 when the accidental fire occurred. [Courtesy of Manchester City Council]*

Fig 3 *The fire-ravaged internal walls of a warehouse in Dale Street. Note the charred wooden lintels to the windows and broken brick work where metal floor-beams have collapsed under the intense heat. [Courtesy of Manchester City Council]*

## 2

# The greatest meer village

'From hence we came on to Manchester, one of the greatest, if not really the greatest meer village in England. It is neither a wall'd town, city, or corporation; they send no members to Parliament ... and yet it has a collegiate church, several parishes, takes up a large space of ground ...'

Daniel Defoe, *A Tour Thro' the Whole Island of Great Britain*, 1724–6

In the popular imagination Manchester is the archetypal industrial and commercial city, a product of the 19th century rising to prominence on the shoulders of King Cotton. What a visitor sees today tends to confirm this view of its origins, but appearances can be deceptive. Manchester has a far longer history, and it was important long before the introduction of powered textile production and the factory system transformed it and its hinterland into one of England's most productive commercial and industrial heartlands.

The Romans built the first Manchester, which they called Mamucium, in the first century AD but little is known of the area from their departure until the 10th century, when there is evidence of a Saxon presence. In the 11th century, William the Conqueror's gift of land to one of his favoured knights triggered the growth of a more significant settlement. Like many medieval English towns it was established on a defensible piece of land at the confluence of two rivers, the Irwell and the smaller Irk. Here the manor house and parish church were sited, but the market place was located a little way to the south. The parish of Manchester was extensive but the medieval town itself was only of local importance, grew slowly and was at first administratively subordinate to Salford across the Irwell. The foundations of its industrial economy were laid in the late middle ages, when the manufacture of woollen and linen cloth was adopted in the town. Cotton was introduced in the 17th century, and by the beginning of the 18th century Manchester was firmly established as a regional centre for the manufacture and trade of cotton goods, and travelling hawkers and salesmen began to make Manchester-made merchandise famous far and wide.

*The Rochdale Canal at Dale Street. The warehouses of the Northern Quarter are in the background. [DP024953]*

The 18th century saw Manchester emerge as a major town, growing in population and expanding both in physical extent and in the reach of its trade and industry (Fig 4). Already, by 1717, its population had grown to about 10,000. Some of the growth was doubtless taken up by more intensive use of space within the old built-up area, but by the early 18th century it was necessary to develop new land to the south of the medieval centre. The St Ann's area, with its classical church of 1709–12 and the adjacent square built in 1720, soon became a fashionable residential neighbourhood, shifting the centre of the town away from its medieval core. In the early 1720s Daniel Defoe, contrasting Manchester's recent physical growth with its otherwise unpretentious character, described the town as 'the greatest meer village in England', although a little later, in 1728, Samuel and Nathaniel Buck described it as 'a spacious and popular [that is, populous] Inland Town'[1]. Further development followed.

As a rising manufacturing and trading town, Manchester depended on transport for the supply of raw materials and access to markets. By 1736 the Rivers Mersey and Irwell had been made navigable between Manchester and the fast-growing port of Liverpool, and later in the 18th century Manchester played a pioneering role in the development of the canal system. One of the earliest canals in England was built by the Duke of Bridgewater in 1765 to carry coal from his mines at Worsley to Manchester and beyond, and the next 40 years saw the development of an extensive canal network with Manchester at its centre, culminating in the completion of the Rochdale Canal in 1804 (*see* p 4). Busy canal basins at Castlefield and at Piccadilly, to say nothing of the numerous canal arms and short branches that were subsequently built, lent the town something of the character of an inland port long before the construction of the Manchester Ship Canal. The canals also made it an attractive location for industry, encouraging the construction of the first steam-powered cotton-spinning mills in Manchester in the 1780s.

Fig 4 *Casson and Bury's plan of Manchester and Salford circa 1710–50. Little of the Northern Quarter, to the upper left of this plan, had yet been built. [Chetham's Library; DP028363]*

1  *Buck, S and N 1728 'The South West Prospect of Manchester, in the County Palatine of Lancaster' reproduced in Hyde, R 1994 A Prospect of Britain: The Town Panoramas of Samuel and Nathaniel Buck. London: Pavillion Books Ltd, Plate 47*

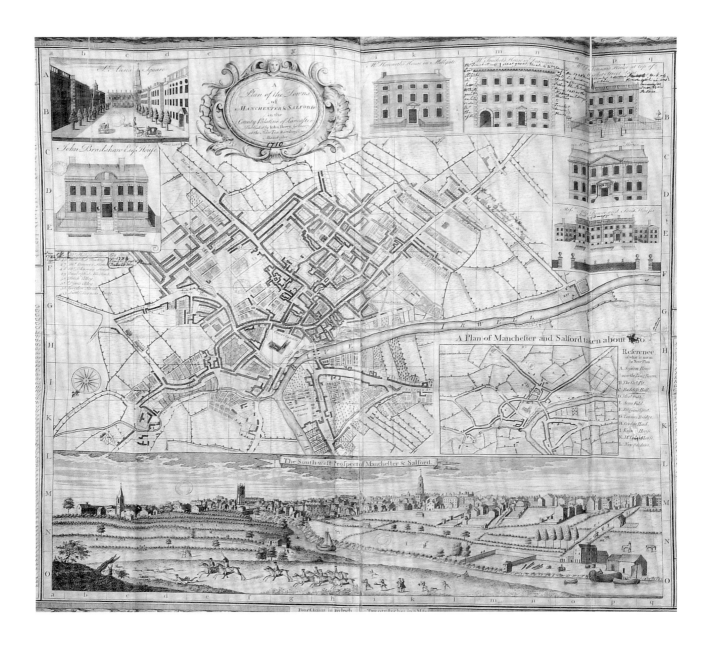

Equally importantly, canal boats brought in the increased quantities of food, fuel and general merchandise needed to support the larger working population attracted by the new factories. By the beginning of the 19th century Manchester's population had risen to approximately 75,000, making it the third most populous town in England.

Manchester might have become a wholly industrialised town of mills and factories during the 19th century but instead commerce burgeoned to such an extent that manufacturing was eclipsed. Aided by good transport links, especially after 1830 with the development of the railway network, the town became the international market place for the produce of hundreds of Lancashire factory towns and villages. Raw cotton was sent out to spinning towns such as Bolton and Oldham, the spun yarn was then dispatched to weaving towns such as Burnley and Nelson – which grew fast after the introduction of powered weaving in the early 19th century – and then Manchester received the finished cloth and marketed it. Manchester's mercantile role was pivotal to the industry, and a new and vibrant commercial district developed. In the centre of the town, mills increasingly gave way to specialist cloth warehouses and offices for manufacturers' agents. Many 18th-century streets were widened and regularised and spacious new streets, such as Whitworth Street, were laid out on the remaining vacant land. Like the industrial landscape of mills and factories on which it depended, the new commercial centre was regarded as a phenomenon of the age. In the 1840s Friedrich Engels noted with amazement how large the new commercial district was, how it consisted almost wholly of offices and towering warehouses, and how, except for patrolling policemen, it was deserted during the night[2].

Manchester's new importance was recognised in 1853, when the town was granted city status. Its industry and economy diversified considerably during the 19th century to include engineering, banking, insurance and retail facilities for the region, and the opening of the

2 *Engels, F 1987* The Condition of the Working Class in England. *(First pub in Germany in 1845, this translation first pub in the USA in 1886) (Penguin Classics). London: Penguin 85–6*

Manchester Ship Canal in 1894 turned the city into a full-scale inland port. The early decades of the 20th century saw commercial activity reach new heights; the cotton exchange, symbol of Manchester's commercial might, was the centre of a global trading network and a new wave of warehouses, banks and office buildings was constructed. In the 1930s, however, the cotton industry entered a period of terminal decline; the region's mills began to close and trade ebbed away. By the 1950s Manchester's cityscape was dominated by an increasingly redundant industrial and commercial legacy of canals and railways, warehouses, office buildings and cotton mills.

Since then Manchester has sought a new identity for itself, and its recent inner-city renaissance is now regarded by many as a model of modern urban regeneration. But rebirth has brought physical change and in many places it is now difficult to appreciate how Manchester looked, worked and developed at different periods in its history. However, within the Northern Quarter the story of Manchester's expansion and changing character can still be read in the landscape and surviving buildings. This small but important area lies to the east of Manchester's medieval core, between the city's Victorian and Edwardian commercial district and the industrial suburb of Ancoats, and is flanked to the east by the Rochdale Canal (*see* p 4). Both influenced and sealed in by these disparate neighbours for more than two centuries, it has evolved a distinctive character of its own as the successive demands of residents, transport, industry and commerce have shaped and re-shaped its built environment.

# 3

# The first Northern Quarter

At the beginning of the 18th century, Manchester was still surrounded by fields and had barely exceeded its medieval boundaries. What later became the Northern Quarter was largely made up of agricultural land on the edge of the town, where the dominant influence was provided by the Lever family, the principal landowner, who had a house there called Lever Hall. The expansion of Manchester began to affect the eastern fringe of the town in the middle of the 18th century (*see* Fig 4). Because land sales to developers within the Northern Quarter were fragmented, leading to piecemeal development, and because construction extended over many decades, during which the opportunities open to builders changed, the area as a whole lacks a uniform character. At first subject to small-scale, unplanned development, later to more concerted schemes introducing new urban forms to the area, and later still to pressures arising from industrial and commercial investment, the Northern Quarter exhibits a highly varied character both in its layout and in the types of buildings constructed.

## Residential development in the 18th century

The first stage of development, in the 1750s and 1760s, saw the expansion of the built-up area of Manchester into the western part of the Northern Quarter. Here new streets – Church Street, Turner Street, Birchin Lane and Union Street – were laid out, not to an overall plan but as the need and opportunity arose (Fig 5). By 1765 the population of this part of the Quarter was large enough to prompt the opening of a church, St Paul's (since demolished), on Turner Street. What drove development was, at least in part, the need to provide new housing for the growing number of workers engaged in the expanding cotton industry. In the mid-18th century cotton working was still a domestic occupation and workers mainly used manually operated machines and tools. Later, from the 1770s, power was successfully applied to yarn production in first water- and then steam-powered mills, but weaving remained a hand-powered operation for many more decades. The great increase in yarn production in the late 18th century naturally led to a commensurate

*12–14 Lever Street, a pair of early 19th-century houses with a warehouse and offices at the rear. [DP028868]*

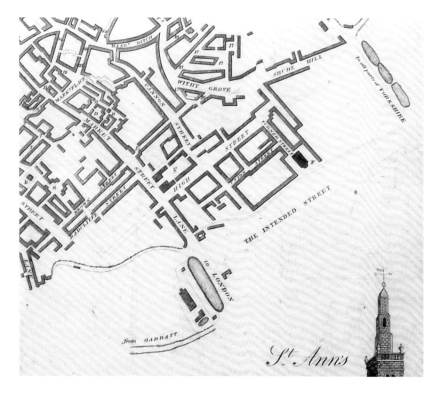

Fig 5 *The extent of the Northern Quarter (to the east of Shude Hill and High Street and to the north of Market Street Lane and the road to London, later Piccadilly) in 1772. [From 'A Plan of Manchester and Salford', Tinker, T 1772 and Fothergill, J 1822; Chetham's Library; DP028365]*

growth in handloom weaving, and Manchester attracted large numbers of weavers, many probably accommodated in the old town. Where new building took place, as in the Northern Quarter, speculators found the construction of housing for weavers an attractive option, for higher rents could be charged both because more space was provided, in the form of weaving rooms, and because, despite trade vicissitudes, weavers were relatively well paid.

It is not clear how many weavers crowded into the Northern Quarter in the last decades of the 18th century, for much early housing has been cleared. Records of buildings made before demolition, and a few surviving houses, however, do provide evidence for the type of accommodation built for, or occupied by, weaving families. Weavers' houses were often built away from the main street frontages, in minor

Fig 6 (above) *Back Turner Street. Although much altered, the former weavers' houses with their characteristically elongated third-floor windows can still be clearly identified. [DP028887]*

Fig 7 (above, right) *84–88 Tib Street. Formerly a terrace of three weavers' houses. Only 88 (shown) retained its original long loomshop window, while 84–86 have been completely demolished. [DP028877]*

lanes such as Back Turner Street, which was lined with them (Fig 6). Here and throughout much of the Northern Quarter were constructed characteristic three-storeyed cottages in terraces or, in some parts, courts. They provided better accommodation than found in the small back-to-back dwellings that accommodated the mill workers and which were built in large numbers in Ancoats and elsewhere in Manchester. Many had cellars, and looms were placed in a loomshop usually in the top storey. Purpose-built weavers' houses are recognisable by the provision of distinctive wide but shallow windows in the front or rear elevations (sometimes both) lighting the loomshop (Fig 7). Sometimes the inclusion of a taking-in door allowed the movement of goods into the loomshop and the removal of the woven cotton cloth directly to the street below; numbers 47–53 Tib Street (Fig 8), a row of three-storeyed houses built in the 1770s, include this feature. Elsewhere, weavers' houses were sometimes built on newly developed principal streets, such as Port Street and Hilton Street, conferring a degree of respectability on the dwellings of the more substantial weavers that is also, surprisingly, apparent in some of those which lined the back lanes: 36 Back Turner Street (Fig 9), for example, was three bays wide and had a frontage of bricks laid in header bond – a prestigious finish. However, weavers' houses on lesser streets were generally meaner, such as 1 Kelvin Street (originally Milk Street) (Fig 10), which retains an early loomshop window frame and the adjacent 3–5 Kelvin Street with which it forms a terrace (Fig 11): these are only one-bay wide and have a shared rear court, originally reached from the street by a covered passage. These remains of a transitional phase in industrial production are

Fig 8 (below, left) *47–53 Tib Street. Note the second-floor taking-in door in the side. [DP028876]*

Fig 9 (below) *36 Back Turner Street before it collapsed in 2005. Note the header-bond brickwork and the orginal three-window arrangement on the first floor. [AA006123]*

Fig 10 (above)  *1–5 Kelvin Street [DP028429].*
*No. 1 retains its original 18th-century workshop*
*window frame* (above, right). *[DP028430]*

highly significant reminders that the first stages of Manchester's
rise to industrial greatness, like those of other great manufacturing
centres such as Birmingham and Sheffield, were based on traditional
hand-powered domestic manufacturing activity, not on the great mills
that dominated later periods.

If the early development of the Northern Quarter was at least in part
motivated by the need to house an industrial workforce and was executed
piecemeal to no overall plan, the next stage was radically different in
character. In many growing industrial towns, late 18th-century expansion
– following London's example – took the form of planned residential
developments, laid out on a grid pattern of streets, sometimes centred
on a square and adorned by the respectable dwellings of increasingly
prosperous manufacturing, commercial and professional families. This
happened first in Bristol with the laying-out of Queen's Square, which
began in 1700, where the fine merchants' houses that faced the square

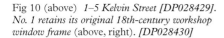

were balanced by warehousing at the rear of their plots, and a number of other squares were subsequently built in prosperous provincial towns and cities throughout the 18th century. Manchester had witnessed such developments early in the century in St Ann's and then St James's Squares, but the release of land for building in the Northern Quarter from the early 1770s offered the chance to repeat the experiment in suburban town planning. Precipitated when Sir Ashton Lever started to sell off part of his estate here, Lever's Row (now Piccadilly) was soon lined with fine houses. Built on the north side of the road, they enjoyed views over the Manchester Infirmary (now demolished) and its fashionable gardens (Fig 12), a valuable piece of open ground in the fast-growing town. The one surviving house from this period, 47 Piccadilly (Fig 13), a substantial dwelling of three storeys, is very different in quality and appearance from the contemporary purpose-built weavers' houses and, although now rendered and bearing a modern ground-floor shop front, it provides a glimpse of what

Fig 11 (opposite) *Cutaway reconstruction based on 1–5 Kelvin Street showing the arrangement of living and working quarters.*

Fig 12 *The Infirmary, Dispensary and Lunatic Asylum circa 1830. The three-storeyed townhouses that once lined the north side of Piccadilly, originally known as Lever's Row, can be seen on the left. [Manchester Archives and Local Studies, m74667; DP028370]*

Fig 13  *47 Piccadilly (centre), an 18th-century house now dwarfed by later structures. The north side of Piccadilly was once lined with houses like this one (see Fig 12). [DP028500]*

was once one of the best and most fashionable residential streets in the town.

An opportunity for a spectacular residential development in the Northern Quarter was permitted by Sir Ashton Lever's sale, in 1780, of a 25-acre (10-hectare) parcel of land making up most of the eastern half of the Quarter beyond the River Tib, a small stream that caused occasional annoyance by bursting its banks until 1783 when it was culverted and Tib Street was created. The area provided prime, unobstructed building land on the edge of the growing town and the buyer was William Stevenson, a local landowner turned speculator. Stevenson made a good start, laying out a grid of streets of different widths. At the centre of the development and at the crossing point of two grand thoroughfares, Great Lever Street and Hilton Street, he placed a square bearing his name. Around this nucleus lesser streets were set out in a clear hierarchy of widths, providing a formal and regular urban landscape (Fig 14) very different from the old centre of Manchester. Principal roads such as Great Lever Street were lined with the largest houses, lending elegance and style to the fast-growing suburb: 8 Lever Street (Fig 15) is one of the best houses in the Quarter, a five-bay, double-fronted house of three storeys with a classical

Fig 14 (below) *William Stevenson's estate as it was laid out in the 1780s. [After Christopher Chalklin]*

Fig 15 (below, right) *8 Lever Street was built between 1780 and 1793 and is one of a number of fine houses of this date that survive in the Northern Quarter. [DP028867]*

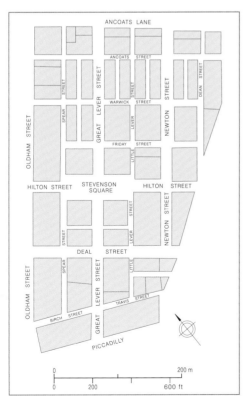

doorcase. In contrast, poorer dwellings were, in the main, confined to lesser lanes such as Bradley Street (*see* p 24). Provision was made for religious observance through the construction in 1781 of a Methodist Chapel, in a grand Georgian-Gothic style on Oldham Street, which replaced the earlier chapel on Birchin Lane, and in 1793 the building of St Clement's Church (Fig 16) on Stevenson Square.

But if the potential of Stevenson's scheme was great and initial plans ambitious, the overall execution lacked cohesion. Even though the construction of handsome town houses continued in the Northern Quarter until the early 19th century, with the building of good surviving examples such as 12–14 Lever Street (*see* p 10), a pair of three-storeyed rendered brick houses with classical doorcases, and 2 Union Street (Fig 17), development faltered, and rapidly changing conditions in and around the Stevenson's area led to a much more mixed character than might have been first envisaged. Ironically, the downfall of the scheme was linked to an overall rise in the fortunes of the town, for the decades after 1780 witnessed a building boom in Manchester that undermined the intended middle-class development of Stevenson Square and steered it instead towards the working classes. The destabilising effect of the boom was exacerbated by the means of regulation, for instead of exercising strict control over building through the use of covenants and retention of the freehold, Stevenson appears to have sold off relatively small parcels of land, with no restrictions, to individual builders or developers. This arrangement contributed to a slow rate of progress and also made it difficult to achieve any degree of uniformity or overall planning – apart from the square there was no specific provision of public open space and few of the houses, even the better-quality ones, appear to have had gardens or even substantial yards. By the end of the 18th century there were still many vacant plots and even Stevenson Square, the intended jewel in the crown, was never coherently developed for middle-class residential use, as demonstrated by the relatively late addition of St Clement's Church. It was ultimately given over to mixed industrial and commercial use (Fig 18), St Clement's being demolished in about 1878. The hierarchy of streets in the development also led to an uncomfortable proximity of wealth and poverty: the building of back-to-back cottages on Stevenson

Fig 16 *St Clement's Church, Stevenson Square, as drawn in 1835 by R Loxham. This church was demolished in about 1878. [Manchester Archives and Local Studies, m70287; DP028377]*

Fig 17  *2 Union Street: an architecturally imaginative house of three bays and three storeys, distinguished by its large, round-headed central doorway and, unusually for such a fine house, its diminutive situation on a back street. For many years in the 19th and 20th centuries it was the Bull's Head public house. [DP028505]*

Place, for example, was not calculated to attract the best residents to the nearby Stevenson Square regardless of the presence of a church.

The failure of Stevenson's scheme as a polite residential suburb was made certain by the changing character of the Northern Quarter. The construction from the 1780s onwards of a canal corridor and associated cotton-spinning mills in neighbouring Ancoats trapped Stevenson's middle-class housing between an industrial suburb and a crowded town centre, and the Northern Quarter began to lose its attraction as an elegant place of residence. Industry began to encroach on the area and by 1800 it contained several cotton mills, one of them, Houldsworth's Newton Street Mill, a giant of seven storeys. It is possible that 39 Hilton Street (Fig 19), now called Marlsbro House, was also among them: there by 1830, it is four storeys high and 16 bays long – its size

Fig 18  *Stevenson Square. The square was laid out in the 1780s and originally intended as a middle-class residential area with an elegant church, but economic changes in the early 19th century meant that it was soon given over to industry and commerce.* *[DP028440]*

and outward appearance suggesting its origins as a cotton mill, especially the front elevation which resembles that of New Mill (built in 1804 and part of Murray's Mills in Ancoats) in that the central four bays project slightly forward. Although not fireproof, its slow-burning internal structure, which consists of single rows of slender cast-iron columns directly supporting spine beams and plank floors, is not inconsistent with this interpretation.

Furthermore, industrial development both in Ancoats and within the area made the Northern Quarter attractive territory for housing the

Fig 19 *39 Hilton Street, now known as Marlsbro House, may have originated in the late 18th century as a cotton-spinning mill. Its 20th-century chequerboard render hides a plain red-brick exterior. [DP028407]*

swelling numbers of mill workers and domestic weavers. There is, therefore, some continuity to be observed between the 1770s, when numerous weavers' cottages were erected in the west of the area, and the decades of the later 18th century and the early 19th century, which were marked by a new wave of house building. The phased construction of 69–77 Lever Street in the 1780s (Fig 20), and the further rapid development of the rest of the plots they occupied, illustrates this period of change (Fig 21). The development was built by a plasterer, William Bradley, but only one of the original houses was intended as a townhouse for a single household. Rising demand for cheaper housing meant that the others, although built almost immediately afterwards, appear to have been designed as tenement houses – some of them with top-floor loomshops, here relegated to the rear of the house to maintain a genteel façade to prestigious Lever Street (Fig 22). Two-storeyed extensions, for independent occcupation, were added to the rears of 69–75 shortly afterwards, and by the mid-1790s even more accommodation had been provided in the form of a row of meagre two-room cottages, some with a cellar, at the rear, fronting Bradley Street.

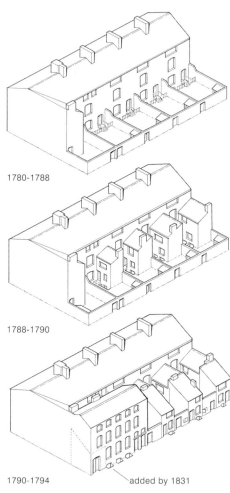

1780-1788

1788-1790

1790-1794          added by 1831

Fig 20 (left) *69–77 Lever Street after reconstruction during the 1990s. [DP028873]*

Fig 21 (above) *69–77 Lever Street originally had open rear yards but these were soon built on as demand for more housing and factory space grew, as this sequence shows.*

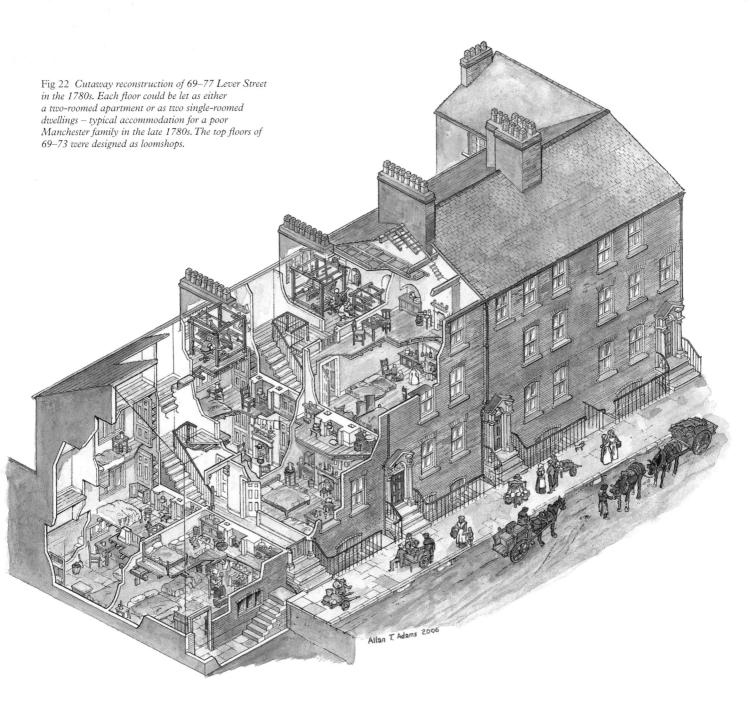

Fig 22 *Cutaway reconstruction of 69–77 Lever Street in the 1780s. Each floor could be let as either a two-roomed apartment or as two single-roomed dwellings – typical accommodation for a poor Manchester family in the late 1780s. The top floors of 69–73 were designed as loomshops.*

Allan T. Adams 2006

Although weaving and other domestic elements of textile manufacture persisted well into the 19th century, technological advances increasingly drew many processes into the factory environment. Use of the power loom, first introduced in 1785, had initially been limited, early examples being slow and unreliable, but by the 1820s many cotton manufacturers had installed them in their factories. Even before this, manufacturers had increasingly dispensed with the services of domestic handloom weavers, whose work and wages dwindled as a consequence. Inevitably many of Manchester's domestic weavers spiralled downwards into poverty, provoking a general mood of popular anger and discontent that was exploited by contemporary political reformers with, in the case of the Peterloo Massacre of 1819, tragic results. The prosperity of the Northern Quarter, with its many weavers, must also have suffered and although it never degenerated as badly as some districts of Manchester, such as Irk Town and Little Ireland, many of its inhabitants no doubt fell on hard times and were forced to live in the kinds of squalid and overcrowded conditions that shocked many contemporaries.

One response to the plight of the poor was the opening of the Manchester Union Industrial Workhouse on Tib Street. Converted from a former corn mill, it was established as an expedient following the Poor Law Amendment Act of 1834, which aimed to regulate eligibility for poor relief more tightly. It was soon replaced by a purpose-built structure in Crumpsall, although the building it previously occupied appears to have survived until at least 1931. Spiritual provision, significantly by the non-conformists, also increased and new chapels, all now gone, were built by the Baptists in Oak Street and on Oldham Street (Bethesda Chapel), while the Methodists opened a further chapel in Lever Street in 1848.

## The rise of commerce and industry

As the Northern Quarter's domestic weaving industry declined during the first half of the 19th century, other, more diverse, industrial ventures thrived as the inhabitants sought new sources of income and employment. Many houses, no longer generating worthwhile income

Figs 23 and 24 *The City and Castle public houses on Oldham Street were both built in the late 18th century as private houses. The City was formerly known as The King's Arms Public House and Coronation Vaults, and the central panels show the arrival of William and Mary, welcomed by Britannia, and the Royal Arms.* [DP028496 and DP028492]

from rents, were converted to commercial premises, including public houses such as The City and the Castle on Oldham Street (Figs 23 and 24). Industrial activity became more prominent in the area, for many new factories were built on the remaining vacant plots. By the 1840s the Northern Quarter was home to engineering and iron works, clothing

factories and timber yards as well as such textile factories as Taylor's
thread-winding mill on Stevenson Square (Fig 25). A major complex of
basins and wharfs was also established around the junction of the Ashton
and Rochdale Canals, to the immediate east of the Northern Quarter,
and several large canal warehouses were built to handle the vast quantity
of merchandise that passed through it. Only two now survive, converted
to new uses, although both are significant examples of their type:
Dale Warehouse (1806), also known as Carver's Warehouse, and
Jackson's Warehouse (1836) (Figs 26 and 27).

Fig 25  *Taylor's Mill, Stevenson Square. Built as a
winding mill for cotton and silk thread in the second
quarter of the 19th century, it retains its former engine
house at the rear. [DP028869]*

Figs 26 and 27  *Dale Warehouse, also known as Carver's Warehouse (right) of 1806 and Jackson's Warehouse (below) of 1836 were both built close to Dale Street by the Rochdale Canal Company. Both warehouses are shown prior to restoration. [DP028448 and AA022353]*

# 4

# A maturing city district and the railway age

The regional canal system had enabled Manchester to develop as an industrial and commercial town, linking it and its neighbours with the port of Liverpool, through which its imports and exports mostly passed. However, it was the development of the railway network in the mid-19th century, combined with advances in manufacturing technology, which really provided the catalyst that would transform Manchester from a regional textile centre into an internationally important commercial city. As Manchester expanded, the Northern Quarter, which was ideally placed to take advantage of the developing railway network and the changes it brought, was transformed from a peripheral residential and industrial suburb into an important central district, and although much of its resident population drained away to newer and more distant suburbs it acquired many new and more important roles. The construction of Manchester's first railway line, the Manchester to Liverpool Railway which opened in 1830, was spurred by the town's dependence on Liverpool's port facilities combined with the relative slowness of canal transport. The railway proved a great success and in the following decades the network expanded at a furious pace. New termini were built and by 1850 there were major railway stations on three sides of the Northern Quarter: Oldham Road goods station, Victoria passenger station and London Road passenger and goods stations, which later became Piccadilly Station.

## A natural market place

The Northern Quarter's location in relation to transport systems made it the natural marketing centre for the growing city. The medieval market place was situated to the south of the town and had served until the 18th century, when the expanding town outgrew its capacity. To compensate, a number of smaller, specialised street markets had grown up across the town and these continued to serve until the early 19th century. However, they evidently proved an undesirable alternative to a single large market and Sir Oswald Mosley, the lord of the manor, determined to consolidate them all in one place in an early attempt at regulation. To this end he

*In the 1870s the High Street was extended to reach Smithfield Market, as this photograph of 1929 shows. [Manchester Archives and Local Studies, m75601]*

leased, from the Earl of Derby, the future Smithfield market site, which was then a cluster of gardens at the north end of the Northern Quarter, because it was open land conveniently close to existing transport links, in the form of the long-established Oldham Road and the Rochdale Canal and its basins to the east, and the town centre to the west and south. Mosley drained and levelled the site, and in 1820 moved the potato market there, followed in 1821 by the butchers', greengrocers' and meal and flour markets. It was officially named 'Smithfield Market' in 1822 and ten years later it consisted of a large open space with the shambles (butchers' market) in one corner, a piazza and the manor office. Smithfield Market continued to grow and soon had special areas for provisions and fruit, a covered shambles, and buildings to house the potato and cheese markets, as well as a night asylum for the destitute. At a time of shortages and poverty, the establishment of the market, and the trade its presence generated, must have done much locally to offset the worst of the hardship caused by the decline of handloom weaving.

The arrival of the railways consolidated the importance of the Northern Quarter in the provisioning of the growing city. By the middle of the 19th century much of the town's food was entering through nearby Oldham Road Station, which, although originally a mixed passenger and goods station, yielded its passenger traffic to Victoria Station in 1844. The increased food supply needed to be managed and the old manorial administration was evidently deemed unsuitable for the task because in 1846 Manchester Corporation purchased the town's market rights from the Mosley family and immediately enlarged Smithfield. A succession of major expansions followed (Fig 28): in about 1850 further land to the east, between Coop Street and Oak Street, was acquired and the layout of the market was rationalised – the wholesale and retail traders being more clearly grouped together. The finest improvement came in 1853–4 when the market area was roofed over in four vast and majestic avenues of cast iron and glass (Fig 29), built by Mr Wheeldon of Derbyshire under the supervision of William Fairbairn, the great Manchester-based engineer. Smithfield Market Hall (Fig 30), essentially a new butchers' hall, followed in 1857–8 to designs by Isaac Holden. One of Smithfield's few surviving structures, it is classically styled and built of stone with Corporation

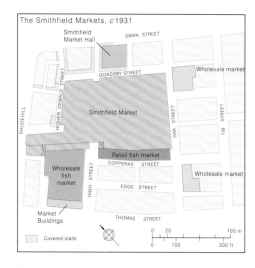

Fig 28 *The extent of Smithfield Market by the 1930s. Most of the expansion took place in the second half of the 19th century. Coop Street has been obliterated by the expansion of the market. (Based on the 1931 Ordnance Survey 1:2500 map.)*

Fig 29 (right) *Smithfield Market in 1854.*
*[Manchester Archives and Local Studies, m59672;*
*DP028376]*

Fig 30 (below) *Smithfield Market Hall from Swan*
*Street. [DP006014]*

MACKIE | MAYOR | 1858

regalia and a carved bull and rams' head in relief on the elevations to both Swan Street and the rest of Smithfield Market (Fig 31). It originally had an open inner courtyard, but this was roofed in 1868 – the structure supported by magnificently decorated octagonal cast-iron columns (Fig 32). In 1865 a separate retail fish market was built adjoining Copperas Street, on the far side of the market. This was later doubled in length to reach Oak Street and it is this portion which survives, and in 1873 it was joined by a large wholesale fish market, situated between High Street and Salmon Street, of which only the outer walls and a single row of cast-iron columns remain. The High Street elevation, which faced the approach

Fig 31 *Part of the market-side elevation of Smithfield Market Hall. The bull's and rams' heads reflect the building's origins as a butchers' hall. [DP006011]*

Fig 32 (opposite) *The interior of Smithfield Market Hall. This area was originally open but was roofed over in 1868. [DP004591]*

to Smithfield Market from the south-west, was enriched by four carved stone tableaux depicting various aspects of the fishing trade (*see* Front cover). In 1878 Market Buildings, a block of commercial chambers, was built beside the Wholesale Fish Market, and the 1870s also saw the extension of High Street through to Smithfield Market (*see* p 30), linking it directly with Market Street.

The population and buildings of the Northern Quarter were affected by railway traffic in other ways. The area was well positioned to take advantage of the increased passing trade generated by the nearby passenger termini. Piccadilly, especially that part which faced the Infirmary, had been the prime street in the area for hotels in the first half of the 19th century, and the opening of London Road Station no doubt influenced the establishment of several others, including the Adelphi Hotel, a substantial five-storeyed classical building, and the Brunswick Hotel, which was opened in converted houses fronting Piccadilly and Paton Street. Hotels, public houses and eating places were also opened on several of the other main streets in the area in the mid-19th century, as well as close to the ever-expanding Smithfield Market. Many, like the Brunswick and the former King Richard the Third on High Street, followed earlier trends and were established in converted houses.

While the transient population was expanding the resident population was contracting. Railways and other forms of public transport (omnibuses from the 1820s, and trams from the 1860s) facilitated the growth of more distant suburbs which drew the former inhabitants, or at last those who could afford it, away from the Northern Quarter. As the residents moved out, the need for local places of worship diminished to the detriment of most of the area's earlier chapels and churches, none of which survive. However, the area's changing character was reflected in the construction of a different type of religious building designed to serve more than a local congregation. The Methodist Central Hall of 1855–6 (Fig 33), built on the site of Oldham Street Chapel, incorporated a small chapel for the dwindling congregation, but its principal component was a large general hall for district meetings and similar events. It also included smaller function rooms and even ground-floor shops intended to provide a maintenance income for the building.

Fig 33 *The severely classical Methodist Central Hall of 1855–6 by George Woodhouse of Bolton. The Hall, which continues to serve the needs of Manchester's Methodists, was damaged by an incendiary bomb in 1941 and was partially rebuilt in 1953–4. [DP028480]*

## The dominance of commerce

The changes that occurred in the Northern Quarter from the mid-19th century were also linked with the changing nature of the Lancashire cotton industry. Rail transport encouraged the dispersal of manufacturing to the satellite mill towns that had already begun to emerge following the earlier expansion of the canal system. Manchester itself was transformed from just another manufacturing town into the undisputed commercial capital of the region, and many central districts were consequently stripped of houses and factories to make way for warehouses, offices and banks (Fig 34). The Northern Quarter developed

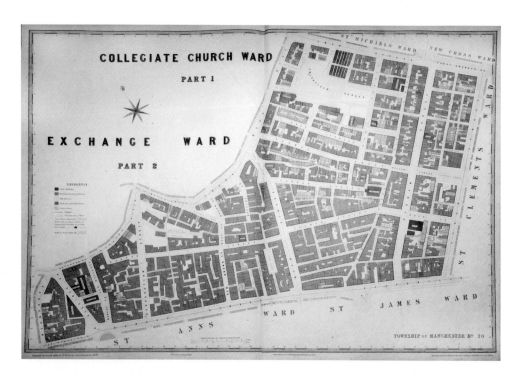

Fig 34 *Joseph Adshead's maps of Exchange Ward (top) and St Clements Ward (bottom), corrected in 1850 and published in 1851, show that warehouses and business premises (coloured medium grey) dominated the Northern Quarter at this time. [Chetham's Library; DP028368 and DP028378]*

to form part – albeit a peripheral part – of a new and very different commercial district. The characteristic building type within this district was the mercantile textile warehouse, and many significant examples were built in the Northern Quarter. Banks and commercial chambers (office buildings) also appeared amongst the warehouses, as did new public houses and eating places such as the Wellington Inn at 33 Back Piccadilly (Fig 35). These buildings were usually much larger than those

Fig 35 *33 Back Piccadilly, formerly the Wellington Inn, was a purpose-built public house, constructed in the 1870s. [DP028862]*

they replaced and many former building plots were often amalgamated to accommodate them. Together they housed a busy, mature and virtually self-supporting commercial community.

The first commercial textile warehouses in the Northern Quarter were established in converted dwellings and many loomshop houses enjoyed a second lease of life in the second quarter of the 19th century in this way. Sometimes the storage capacity of a converted house was later supplemented by the addition of an adjacent, purpose-built warehouse block, and this happened at 48–50 Thomas Street, a pair of late 18th-century houses with top-floor loomshops that had become business premises by 1850, where a warehouse, 7 Kelvin Street, was built on the site of the former rear wings and yards (Frontispiece). But the rapid growth of the trade soon demanded bigger and more specialised premises and for nearly a hundred years, from the mid-19th century until the second quarter of the 20th century, commercial warehouse design continually evolved as the buildings were finely tailored to the specific needs of the Manchester textile trades – office space, storage space, display space, making-up space, and efficient loading facilities. Combining lively public façades with contrastingly drab service elevations, the new warehouses artfully compacted under one roof carefully designed public and private circulation areas, offices, warerooms, inspection rooms and loading bays – either in the form of full-height loading slots (recessed, single-bay tiers of taking-in doors) or internal ground-floor vehicle bays known locally as hovels.

In the 1840s, in the Northern Quarter, many of the fine houses that once lined Piccadilly began to be replaced with equally fine, but much larger, warehouses, such as the Italianate 49 Piccadilly, built in 1846–7 (Fig 36). At five storeys high it presents an imposing façade to Piccadilly while the rear elevation, to Back Piccadilly, incorporates two internal hovels with monumental round-headed rusticated surrounds. Then, as Manchester's commercial district encroached further and further into the Northern Quarter during the second half of the 19th century and early 20th century, more warehouses were built, especially in and around Dale Street, Piccadilly, Newton Street, Hilton Street, and in the vicinity of Stevenson Square. The new warehouses varied greatly in architectural

Fig 36  *49 Piccadilly, an Italianate warehouse of the 1840s. [DP028866]*

style and size: some, like 33 Dale Street (Fig 37) and 18–20 Hilton Street (Fig 38), were plain to the point of austerity, while others, by the 1850s, had adopted the fashionable palazzo style, alluding to the past supremacy of Italy's merchant cities and associating the basis of Manchester's economy with the glories of earlier mercantile empires. Later, in the 1860s and 1870s, the trend turned to more overtly Gothic influences as illustrated at 75–77 High Street, built in the 1870s (Fig 39). The end of the 19th century also saw significant advances in building technology, which were put to good use in new warehouses. The introduction of iron,

Fig 37  *33 Dale Street was probably built in the 1850s as a shipping warehouse. [DP028896]*

Fig 38 (above) *18–20 Hilton Street is one of a group of warehouses built in the third quarter of the 19th century surrounding an open inner yard. [DP028872]*

Fig 39 (right) *75–77 High Street, a clothing warehouse of the 1870s built in an elaborate Venetian Gothic style. [DP028894]*

and later steel, framing meant that the buildings could be constructed with ever more storeys, while the opening of the Manchester Ship Canal in 1894 increased the need for larger warehouses with more storage capacity and better loading arrangements. Examples include Sevendale House, 7 Dale Street (Fig 40), built in 1903–6 for I J & G Cooper Ltd to designs by J Bowden, which occupies an entire block, as does the more secluded Fourways House, 16–18 Tariff Street, built in 1906, which is a large packing, shipping and home-trade warehouse.

The purpose-built commercial warehouses of the later 19th and early 20th centuries had a tremendous impact on the grain of the streets. They were much larger than the domestic structures they replaced and they occupied amalgamated building plots. The eastern half of Dale Street (Fig 41), once known as Clowes Street, is particularly impressive. Dale

Fig 40  *Sevendale House, built for I J & G Cooper Limited, a firm of drapers, in 1903–6. [DP028871]*

Fig 41 *The eastern half of Dale Street; the Dale canal warehouse of 1806 is to the right with the warehouses of F W Millington and J D Williams to the left. [DP028474]*

Street connected the Northern Quarter with the wharfs and basins of the Rochdale and Ashton canal junction and more importantly, from 1865, with the Manchester, Sheffield and Lincolnshire Railway's goods station, which was situated between the canals and the earlier London Road Station. Advantageously positioned, it became lined with large, imposing textile warehouses including 64–66, a merchants' warehouse of 1871; Eleska House, a small clothing warehouse of early 20th-century date; Langley Buildings, a mail-order warehouse built for J D Williams & Co in 1908–9; and Industry House (Fig 42), built in 1912 for Fred W Millington, a manufacturer's agent. Interestingly many of the later Dale Street warehouses were constructed over and around a series of elongated courts and private lanes, formed either by gating off former residential side streets or by creating new service roads such as Lizard Street, which now links Dale Street with Hilton Street. In 1849 the site of Lizard Street

Fig 42 *Warehouse for Fred W Millington on Dale Street designed by W. Longworth of Manchester and approved by the city in February 1912. [Reproduced by courtesy of Chief Executives Department, Manchester City Council, AA026891]*

was occupied by a timber yard but by the end of the century it was flanked by warehouses and in 1902 a new U-shaped range was built across its Hilton Street end with a gated central archway controlling access (Fig 43).

In Dale Street, as elsewhere in Manchester such as Princess Street and Whitworth Street, there can be no mistaking the nature of the local economy. However, unlike the centre of the commercial district, not all of the earlier houses were removed as the local economy changed, and in places 18th-century dwellings still stand side by side with towering warehouses in this part of the Northern Quarter, as if to emphasise the sweeping changes that had taken place in the course of a century (Fig 44).

Fig 43 (right) *30–32 Hilton Street was built as warehouses and offices in 1902. The entrance in the centre of the left-hand elevation opens into Lizard Street. [DP028403]*

Fig 44 (below) *Hilton Street. Small 18th-century houses and large multi-storeyed Victorian and Edwardian warehouses rub shoulders in many parts of the Northern Quarter. [DP024958]*

The last major phase of warehouse building in the Northern Quarter came in the 1920s and 1930s when a number of large wholesale drapery warehouses were built, close to the developing retail district around Market Street and the southern ends of High Street, Oldham Street and Tib Street. Steel-framed, they utilised large areas of glass in their side elevations, while their frontages reflected the architectural idioms of the day. Pall Mall House, 14–22 Church Street (later known as The Coliseum), was built in 1928 as a wholesale warehouse by the Pall Mall Property Company to designs by Jones, Francis and Dalrymple (Fig 45). At ten storeys high it is a huge, T-plan building and has a giant classically styled frontage with a glass curtain from the second to the fifth floor. The most impressive warehouse of this period is, however, the monumental Rylands Building on Market Street. Built for the old textile firm of Rylands and Sons Ltd in 1930–32, it was designed by P Garland Fairhurst, with the help of his father (the famous Manchester warehouse architect Harry S Fairhurst), and subsequently became a department store. The Rylands Building has a steel frame clad with Portland stone, in what was then called the 'modern style', its design influenced by contemporary American structures. It remains one of the most striking buildings in Manchester (Fig 46).

Banks did not appear in the Northern Quarter until the second half of the 19th century, following the success of Smithfield Market and the encroachment of the main commercial district into the area. Most were branch offices, occupying just the ground floors of buildings otherwise used for different purposes, such as 79 High Street, a branch of the Manchester and Salford Bank, which occupied the corner of Market Buildings, a block of commercial chambers built in 1878 (Fig 47). Commercial chambers, in contrast, were usually purpose-built. They were often speculative ventures, rather than premises for a specific firm, and the tenants could be quite diverse, not all having close ties with the textile trades: among the other tenants who occupied Market Buildings in the 1880s, for example, were a government tax officer, an auctioneer, an umbrella manufacturer and a fancy goods agent. However, by this time every significant firm in the Lancashire cotton industry had its representative or agent firmly established in Manchester, and because

Fig 45  *Pall Mall House, 14–22 Church Street, latterly known as The Coliseum. The warehouse is shown prior to conversion.* [DP028503]

Fig 47 *Market Buildings, Thomas Street, commercial chambers of 1878. [DP028893]*

Fig 46 (opposite) *The Rylands Building, Market Street and High Street, by P Garland Fairhurst, 1930–32. [DP028501]*

they did not need warehouse space they operated from commercial chambers. Usually sited on main roads or close to Smithfield Market, these structures almost always incorporated ground-floor shops to provide extra income for the owners. Sometimes they were situated on corner plots, where they might have more than one impressive show elevation and where they could also maximise the amount of natural light entering the premises. In layout they generally followed a common pattern: one or more external doorways would open on to a staircase, and later a lift, which ascended the full height of the building, with a corridor on each floor serving individual offices.

Commercial chambers varied in size and architectural style, reflecting, like the warehouses with which they rubbed shoulders, the length of time over which they were built. The earliest that survives is

31–35 Goadsby Street (*see* Fig 67), built in the 1860s. At three storeys high it is also one of the smallest, although highly ornamented, and contrasts markedly with later monsters such as St Margaret's Chambers, 1–11 Newton Street, built in 1889 (Fig 48). Styles included 31–35 Goadsby Street's High Victorian Gothic and the Gothic and Elizabethan styling of the stone-fronted 55–57 Piccadilly, which although four storeys

Fig 48 *St Margaret's Chambers, 1–11 Newton Street, commercial chambers of 1889. [DP028897]*

high is dwarfed by its neighbour, the six-storeyed Jacobean and Baroque Clayton Buildings, 59–61 Piccadilly, of 1907–9. In contrast, 1 Piccadilly, built in 1879, has novel cast-iron framed elevations to Piccadilly and Tib Street (Fig 49). These elaborate frontages were usually combined with purely functional rear elevations: St Margaret's Chambers, for example, have a much simpler elevation to Back Piccadilly than the showy eight-bay frontage with its four enormous shaped gables (*see* Fig 48). Although the functions of commercial chambers were usually distinct from the functions of warehouses, some commercial chambers were also designed with warehousing space. When its design was approved in 1877, 77–83 Piccadilly was described as 'Shops, warehouse & offices' and for this reason it has a tier of taking-in doors at the rear. Similarly 69–75 Piccadilly has three cranes mounted on its rear elevation – demonstrating the symbiotic relationship between commercial chambers and the more powerful symbol of Manchester as Cottonopolis – the commercial textile warehouse.

Fig 49  *1 Piccadilly, iron-framed shops and commercial chambers of 1879 by J H Lynde. [DP028483]*

**5**

# An economy in flux

The proliferation of wholesale textile warehouses in the Northern Quarter during the 19th century was to some extent balanced by the area's simultaneous emergence as one of Manchester's main retail centres. It is hard now for the casual observer to appreciate that by the beginning of the 20th century Oldham Street probably contained more clothing shops than any similar street in the city, and that for Manchester's women it was claimed to be the hub of the local universe.[1] By the 1950s retailing was more important to Manchester's economy than the wholesale trades, which fell into terminal decline in the 1930s. The Northern Quarter, which contained both the city's most important shopping street and its main market, was particularly important.

## Shops and the retail trade

The nature of the Northern Quarter's shops evolved slowly over two centuries. They must have existed on many of the streets which spread across the area during the 18th century, as part of the general urban scene, but none of the earliest, many of which would have been contrived in existing domestic buildings, survives. The first purpose-built shops were also small and generally resembled houses, but during and after the mid-19th century it became more common for them to have characterful and eye-catching façades, which altered the appearance of Manchester's principal shopping streets. By this time Oldham Street, a major thoroughfare and long-established approach to Manchester, had emerged as one of the city's prime shopping locations. From the late 18th century it had accumulated a broad range of shops, which later became dominated by haberdashers and drapers. As early as the beginning of the 19th century it was home to a number of competing drapery firms and later, in 1867, it was reported that almost every building was either a shop or a public house, more so even than on Deansgate which, as an early approach to the town, has always been one of Manchester's most important streets.

*87 Oldham Street, the eye-catching upper floors of the former premises of Henry Jacob, tailor and outfitter. [DP028490]*

1 *Swindells T 1907* Manchester Streets and Manchester Men *(2nd series). Manchester: Cornish 135*

In the second half of the 19th century Oldham Street contained a number of large tailoring concerns, including that of Henry Jacob, who built an eye-catching, three-storeyed shop in Italianate style at No. 87 (*see* p 54). There were also many so-called mourning warehouses, such as 26 Oldham Street (Fig 50), designed to accommodate a wide range of black, ready-made clothing goods suitable for the period of public mourning following a personal bereavement. The term 'warehouse', as used here, had been commonly used to describe large shops since the second half of the 18th century and did not necessarily imply a wholesale function. One of the most important retailing concerns was Affleck and Brown, a particularly successful drapery firm, which began business at 59 Oldham Street in the 1850s. It went on to take over many other shops before rebuilding 49–61 Oldham Street (*see* Fig 68) as a huge drapery emporium in 1879. On the ground floor such shops had counters and showrooms while the first floors were used as showrooms, and for this reason many incorporated full-width ornamented first-floor windows, often of cast iron (Fig 51; *see also* Fig 50). This was a common feature of shops in England at this time and was especially favoured by businesses selling drapery, furniture and ironmongery. Such an arrangement represented a good use of space in properties with a restricted ground plan, spreading income-earning over more than one level. Other floors would have contained stockrooms, workrooms and, in some cases, living accommodation. By the beginning of the 20th century property speculators were capitalising on the retail boom and constructing large, purpose-built shop premises, often with more than one tenant in mind. The building at 28–40 Oldham Street (Fig 51), for example, was designed to house, among others, a drapers and mourning warehouse, a manufacturer of mantles (shawls) and a cabinet maker. Designed in 1901–2 by Andrews and Butterworth and completed in 1905, it is an impressive structure of three storeys with prestige elevations to Oldham Street and Hilton Street incorporating ground-floor shop windows and display windows above (Fig 52).

To the north-west of Oldham Street, the environs of Smithfield Market also became, not surprisingly, a honey pot for shopkeepers and retailers as well as publicans and hoteliers who relied not only on the

Fig 50 *26 Oldham Street, Paling & Co's former mourning warehouse. Note the arcaded first-floor display window. [DP028881]*

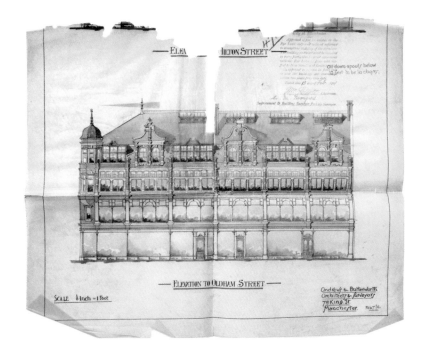

Fig 51  *28–40 Oldham Street. This building-control elevation drawing shows the original design for the Oldham Street elevation. The design for the parapet was later altered. [Reproduced by courtesy of Chief Executives Department, Manchester City Council, DP028373]*

Fig 52  *28–40 Oldham Street. The original first-floor display windows have mostly been replaced. [DP028880]*

thirst of the market workers but on passing trade from shoppers. The shops often differed in design from those built elsewhere, being open fronted, without a glazed shop window, enabling customers to walk in and out at will. This was quite appropriate because in many ways such shops were a functional extension of the Smithfield Market stalls, selling provisions such as fruit, vegetables and fish. When not in use, the fronts of these shops were protected by wooden shutters and later by roller blinds such as those installed from the outset at 46–48 Copperas Street (Fig 53), built in 1927–8 as shops and offices for fish merchants Henry Lever and Sons. The public houses that thrived on market trade included

Fig 53  *46–48 Copperas Street was designed by G H Fletcher and completed in 1928. The ground floor originally had open shop fronts. [DP028895]*

Fig 54 *The Lower Turk's Head pub on Shudehill.*
*[DP024955]*

Fig 55 *The Hare & Hounds pub on Shudehill.*
*[DP028510]*

the Lower Turk's Head (Fig 54), 36 Shudehill, and the Hare & Hounds (Fig 55) – a public house of late 18th-century origin but retaining a fine remodelled interior of the mid-1920s. Many warehouses and small factories were also established close to the market, no doubt attracted to some extent by the lively business environment it offered: one of the most notable examples of the latter survives on the opposite side of Shudehill where William Stovell established an umbrella works and shop (Fig 56).

Fig 56 *Stovells Buildings, an umbrella and walking stick factory and shop of 1900 and 1915, was designed by Thomas Horsfield. [DP028508]*

Built in phases between 1900 and 1915, it is a remarkable building with a distinctive rear elevation that steps back, floor by floor, providing top lighting for the workshops within (Fig 57). As the 20th century progressed, the range of shops in Oldham Street broadened and many earlier premises were rebuilt. Nos 60a and 76–80 Oldham Street, for example, were rebuilt by Lennards, boot makers, and Dobbins, fancy drapers, respectively. Some of these shops still bear their former proprietors' names (Fig 58). Elsewhere 21–31 (Fig 59) and 6–12 Oldham Street, rebuilt in the early 1920s and 1931 respectively, display

Fig 57 *The stepped rear of Stovells Buildings helped to illuminate the workshops within. [DP028509]*

the pretensions of a major international style, for they make use of the giant order, a classical motif that was first used for a shop front by Selfridges in London's Oxford Street in 1909.

The success of the Oldham Street shops naturally attracted branches of the new breed of national chain stores. In the late 1920s, before the refronting of 1931, 6–12 Oldham Street had two tenants: F W Woolworth and Boots, names still familiar today. Marks & Spencer, C&A Modes, Burton, and Swears & Wells also established branches on Oldham Street, and most of the shops they built, often by amalgamating and refronting

older units, still survive. Such firms preferred their stores, wherever they were, to adopt a distinctive corporate architectural style. In 1929 Marks & Spencer converted 46–50 Oldham Street (Fig 60) into a single shop, refronting the whole in artificial stone. The new premises were designed by Marks & Spencer's favoured architect in the north, Norman Jones of Southport, who followed a strict corporate formula that was applied to all the company's shops of this period. Montague Burton, the Leeds firm of

Fig 58 (above, left) *76–80 Oldham Street. This striking shop front was built for Dobbins fancy drapers.* [DP028494]

Fig 59 (above) *21–31 Oldham Street were rebuilt for J Jones, costumiers.* [DP024956]

Fig 60 *Former Marks & Spencer at 46–50 Oldham Street. The frontage was rebuilt in 1929 by the company's architect. [DP028879]*

tailors, built shops at 101–103 Oldham Street (Fig 61) in 1930–31 and opposite at 90–92 in 1933–5, both of them in a uniform art-deco style and designed by their own building department headed by Harry Wilson. Interestingly, Burton's shops, here and elsewhere, were not just used for retailing – upper floors were often given over to billiard rooms, dancing schools, ballrooms and offices, thus earning revenue for the firm from the space not needed by the shop. A large new store was also built for

Fig 61 *101–103 Oldham Street, one of two shops built in Oldham Street in the 1930s for Montague Burton.* [DP028491]

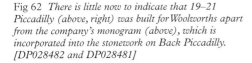

Fig 62 *There is little now to indicate that 19–21 Piccadilly (above, right) was built for Woolworths apart from the company's monogram (above), which is incorporated into the stonework on Back Piccadilly. [DP028482 and DP028481]*

Woolworths at 19–21 Piccadilly, on the corner of Oldham Street, in 1927–9 (Fig 62), and C&A Modes employed London architects North, Robin & Wilsden to design their large store of 1928 at 13–19 Oldham Street (Fig 63). The corporate architecture of the 20th-century chain store, with its tall, wide frontages of glass and artificial stone, changed the face of Oldham Street, giving it the appearance of a sophisticated, modern shopping capital, but not one of the firms that originally built them remains there. Even one of the last, Cantors furniture store of 1961, later became the offices of *The Big Issue in the North*, a self-help magazine sold by the homeless.

Fig 63  *13–19 Oldham Street, formerly C&A Modes.*
*[DP028884]*

## The aftermath of war: optimism, neglect and renewal

The onset of the Second World War had brought with it its own set of priorities. It was a time of austerity and shortages and retailing inevitably suffered. However, at its end the nation was gripped by a new feeling of optimism and the nation looked forward, rather than back, to a brave new future – a mood that was reflected in the architecture of the period. The first modern multi-storeyed office blocks appeared in the Northern Quarter in the late 1950s and sometimes, like commercial chambers of the 19th century, they incorporated ground-floor shops. Nos 24–32 High Street (Fig 64), for example, built in 1959, consisted of a five-storeyed tower over an extensive two-storeyed podium containing shops. Elsewhere Bishopsgate House on Great Ancoats Street, built in 1969,

Fig 64 *24–32 High Street was originally built in 1959 to designs by Leach, Rhodes & Walker.* [DP028502]

Fig 65  *26–28 Hilton Street, Hilton House, designed by Richard Seifert and Partners and built in the early 1960s. [DP028402]*

and Chatsworth House on Lever Street, of 1975, at six and eight storeys high respectively, loomed equally large in the landscape, their brutal style clashing with the earlier structures that surrounded them. But their disproportionate scale was not an entirely new departure – the appearance of the large and architecturally lavish Victorian and Edwardian warehouses would have seemed the same beside the much smaller and architecturally restrained Georgian houses which survived in their shadow. Conversely, some of the smaller structures built in the 1960s, such as Hilton House, 26–28 Hilton Street, of 1961 (Fig 65), are good period examples and less at odds with the scale of their surroundings.

In the 1970s the viability of the Northern Quarter as a retail area, and even as a successful office district, received two devastating blows with the closure of Smithfield Market and the building of the nearby Arndale Centre. Just as the market's presence had benefited its locality, so its removal had an opposite, blighting, effect still evident in nearby Goadsby Street, Copperas Street, Edge Street and Thomas Street. The decline of the area, and of the wider Northern Quarter, was compounded later in the decade by the opening of the Arndale Centre. One of Europe's largest shopping centres when built in 1972–9, this might have consolidated the Northern Quarter's retail function, but instead it defiantly turned its back on the area, facing south onto Market Street and presenting a blind, tiled façade to the north and east. This severed the Northern Quarter from the busy retail traffic of the new centre and quickly a stark contrast developed – on one side a new and seductive shopping area packed with customers, on the other – towards the Northern Quarter – increasingly deserted streets lined with empty shops. By 1980 nearly a quarter of the Northern Quarter's retail tenants had been drawn away, most of them the traders, large and small, from Oldham Street. The malaise also spread to neighbouring Tib Street, once famous for its pet shops, where many of the buildings, abandoned or at best poorly maintained, fell into a semi-derelict state. Even the wholesale clothing trade declined and in some areas many small businesses ultimately closed, leaving whole streets full of empty buildings.

More recently, however, the Northern Quarter has enjoyed a retail revival. In Oldham Street some of the former drapery warehouses and department stores have become home to a new type of alternative shopping complex, the indoor bazaar, the first of which was 'Affleck's Palace', established in the 1980s and laid out with stalls like a market place in a large, late 19th-century shop and warehouse building (Fig 66). Piccadilly continued to profit from its favourable position and even the wholesale clothing trade has retained a significant presence in the warehouses of Dale Street.

These developments could not replace the lost shopping, marketing and commercial functions of the Northern Quarter, however, and by the early 1990s it had become clear that a consolidated strategy for this

Fig 66 *52–54 Church Street, built in the late 19th century and incorporating the structure of a former and earlier public house. Since the 1980s the building has been known as Affleck's Palace and has housed a shopping bazaar. [DP028479]*

under-exploited area, so full of development potential, was needed. In 1993 Manchester City Council officially commissioned a regeneration study in recognition of the Northern Quarter's distinctive local character. Commercial developers, such as Urban Splash who have their origins in the Northern Quarter and employ local architects (for example, Stephenson Bell), have subsequently turned their attention to the area. The Smithfield Building on Oldham Street (*see* Fig 68, p 76) is one of the first such high-profile projects. The turn-of-the-century boom in inner-city living highlighted the potential of the larger warehouses for residential conversion, and many buildings have been altered and put to new uses – a trend that is continuing. This represents a nice completion of the circle, for the Northern Quarter, which had started with such high hopes of developing into a prosperous residential zone, might at last realise this goal in the very different circumstances of a rejuvenated 21st-century Manchester.

# 6

# Conservation and change in the Northern Quarter

## *Julian Holder*

*The Burton Building was originally constructed in 1933–5 as one of Montague Burton's chain of tailoring shops. It has now been enlarged and has a modest rooftop extension to create new flats. [DP028517]*

The Northern Quarter can seem a defensive, even intimidating area nowadays to those who don't know it. Hidden behind a great wall of impressive buildings lining Piccadilly to its south – from Debenhams to the Rossetti Hotel (both conversions from former uses) – along its west by the magnificent ensemble of buildings for the Co-operative Wholesale Society, and to the north by the traffic and buildings of Great Ancoats Street, there are few easy entry points that don't also create an understandable wariness in visitors. Even its most open gateways, at Shudehill and Piccadilly Basin, can make the timid feel they should turn back. But for those who do venture in, the Northern Quarter has many surprises for variety, rather than architectural uniformity, is its predominant characteristic. Overall there are few places where it displays the architectural good manners of its 18th-century residential origins, or the functional consistency of Manchester's better known warehouse districts. Rather than purity, the area presents an arresting hotch-potch of form and function that is at once vital, complex and hybrid – the legacy of a rich multi-layered past. It is a microcosm of Manchester's history, from its early industrial expansion, through its commercial heyday and decline, to a new climate of regeneration. When we consider that Manchester is the world's first industrial city, this marks it out as much more than just another decayed inner-city leftover – it makes its survival remarkable and its heritage-led regeneration of vital importance.

The legacy of the past manifests itself in many ways. The Northern Quarter still contains scattered examples of 18th-century housing, once common in many other parts of Manchester, alongside contrasting concentrations of later offices, shops and warehouses, some of considerable architectural merit. The so-called Cocozza Wood building (Fig 67), standing beside Goadsby Street, is a tour de force of High Victorian Gothic; Langley Buildings present a muscular example of the Baroque Revival of the early 20th century while its neighbour, 38–40 Hilton Street, is a classic example of inter-war Moderne. The juxtaposition of building types and dates – from the grand Victorian markets on the north-west side to the enormous Edwardian warehouses near Piccadilly Station, with a roll-call of mid-20th-century corporate retail architecture dividing the two along Oldham Street – creates an area

Fig 67 *31–35 Goadsby Street, the Cocozza Wood building, mid-19th-century commercial chambers with shops on the ground floor. [DP028465]*

differentiated by scale, materials, density and function from the more homogenous city-centre districts.

The patina of history now hangs heavily on the Northern Quarter, adding a texture and depth that is more than mere bricks and mortar. At the beginning of the 21st century the area is a complex interaction of buildings, spaces and details, redolent with memories and cultural associations – the so-called intangible heritage. For some people the former C&A store will always be associated with Julie Christie making her first screen appearance in the 1963 film 'Billy Liar'. A younger generation might remember the Northern Quarter as the city-centre home of the creative industries during the heyday of 'Madchester', when a vibrant international music industry grew out of an era of industrial decline. Others might fondly recall visits to 'Woolies' on Oldham Street, or tea in the now demolished Ceylon Café on Piccadilly.

Sadly, however, the signs of the area's slow decline over the last 40 years of the 20th century are still all too apparent. By the 1980s and early 90s it was more likely to be thought of as an area of petty crime, sweat shops, absentee landlords and abandoned buildings ripe for wholesale clearance than as a distinctive and vulnerable part of the city's heritage. Once a key component of the city centre, the Northern Quarter lay all but forgotten until 1993, when the first council regeneration study was undertaken. Paradoxically, dereliction has saved the historical integrity of the Northern Quarter and its buildings, though at a cost. Low rental values attracted into the area businesses without the means to maintain important, but otherwise redundant, buildings adequately; other buildings were demolished and many remain at risk (Fig 10, p 15).

## Renaissance

But the familiar consequences of neglect are now balanced by signs of recovery. As the economy of Manchester continues to grow, the Northern Quarter is once again being populated by those who value city-centre living and, thankfully, appreciate the area's individual, counter-cultural nature. When completed in 1998, the refurbishment of the Smithfield Building (Fig 68), Oldham Street, was the first high-profile demonstration that the re-development of the Northern Quarter could be different and it consolidated a re-evaluation of the area initiated by local residents, traders and artists. This trend has been perpetuated by conversions such as 61, Thomas Street (now the offices of Pink Music), recent warehouse conversions along Turner Street and Dale Street, and the new residential developments by Ician on part of the site of the former Smithfield Market. As the area recreates itself, new residents will benefit from the great

Fig 68 *The Smithfield Building, Oldham Street, containing the remains of Affleck and Brown's drapery emporium. [DP028488]*

quantity of facilities for affordable city living that remains – but it needs nursing back to health and new uses need to be found for redundant buildings. If few of them merit meticulous restoration, many deserve careful conservation and then sensitive re-use if the area's distinctiveness is not to be sacrificed. This is a process pioneered earlier in Manchester's Castlefield district, where a mixture of warehouse conversions and complementary new architecture regenerated a former industrial area as a place to live, work and enjoy. Ancoats, the world's first industrial suburb and a close cousin of the Northern Quarter, is also now being transformed into a vital extension of Manchester city centre.

As Castlefield, and now Ancoats, demonstrate, sustaining economic development and conserving the historic environment are not mutually exclusive. Already new developments, such as the flats within the surviving external walls of the 19th-century Wholesale Fish Market (Fig 69), demonstrate how creative architectural responses to the Northern Quarter can work with, and not against, the grain of an area and spur economic regeneration locally. The Wholesale Fish Market

Fig 69 *21st-century development within the Wholesale Fish Market of 1873. [DP028436]*

development is not façadism, for there is no pretence of being anything other than it is, but it knits the old and new together in an exciting and vital manner and connects with the proposed new development area behind the Smithfield Market. Similarly, conversions such as the former Retail Fish Market into the Crafts Gallery, 8 Stevenson Square into retail outlets and 135–141 Oldham Street into the offices of *The Big Issue* have breathed life back into their neighbourhoods. Many of these larger structures can relatively easily find sympathetic new uses, such as the conversion of the Market Buildings on Thomas Street (*see* Fig 47), whilst some lend themselves to more radical interventions, such as the Coliseum, formerly Pall Mall House (*see* Fig 45). Others, such as Newton Buildings and the original Smithfield Market Hall (*see* Figs 30–32), still await similar re-use but are eminently suitable for careful conversion. However, it is the small-scale buildings, treasures such as The Castle public house (*see* Fig 24) or the small back-street warehouses and weavers' houses, that will require special care when changes are proposed.

The area also needs new developments if it is to prosper. Together with our partners in the Commission for Architecture and the Built Environment (CABE), English Heritage has argued for good contemporary interventions being carefully fitted into historic areas as part of this process. Design quality is particularly important where large developments threaten the existing morphology of the area. Where increased density is sought, for example, well-designed and modestly scaled set-back roof-top extensions may be appropriate and, like the Burton Building (*see* p 72) on Oldham Street, or Tib Street apartments, can extend the architectural vocabulary of the area. Unsightly empty plots between buildings also invite good contemporary design.

Ultimately the success of any redevelopment will be measured by how well the authenticity of the area is maintained; this is manifested not only in obvious features such as the street pattern, with its small capillaries such as Kelvin Street and Back Turner Lane, but in details like the art-deco stairlight to 7–9 Swan Street (Fig 70). The challenge for all the parties involved – English Heritage, Manchester City Council, developers, and residents – is to maintain the best of the old and

Fig 70 *The stairlight at 7–9 Swan Street. The survival of incidental details like this adds much to the richness of the Northern Quarter's streetscapes.* [DP028874]

encourage the new, working beneath the skin of the area and setting new developments carefully within the Northern Quarter's maze of streets and back lanes. The process must ensure that any renewal of the Northern Quarter does not result in 'new lamps for old', thereby losing what is intrinsically valuable about the place – its bohemianism and idiosyncrasy that is so attractive to high-quality retailers. This must be managed in a way that maintains the amalgam of different districts, each with its own grain and atmosphere. But this is no urban museum and each district must be defined by what it is, rather than, by default, what it was, and must still have relevance for the future. Dominated until recently by the remnants of the textile industry, it is a working area, loved by many and increasingly being revitalised. It is quite literally turning from rags to riches.

However, unlike the rapid, and sometimes chaotic, developments of earlier centuries we now have the chance to draw breath and consider future developments with the care they deserve. This can be achieved through a variety of formal measures. Detailed understanding of the area's historical development has been provided by the extensive architectural survey that English Heritage research staff undertook between 2000 and 2001. The vision is provided by the Development Framework drawn up by Manchester City Council in 1995, which recognises the unique, varied and independent nature of the area. Then there is the protective legal framework of which listed buildings are the cornerstones. Listing – the legal protection of a building of 'special architectural or historic interest' – does not necessarily mean that a building must be fossilised. Indeed, without adaptation to new uses many of our listed buildings will be condemned to a slow and sad decline. It simply ensures that changes are informed by an understanding of the building and its significance, so that they work with, rather than against, the building's inherent qualities.

The Northern Quarter contains the highest density of listed buildings in the city and many feel that this has been one of the reasons for the area's remarkable survival. They lie within two Conservation Areas – Smithfield and Stevenson Square – both designated by Manchester City Council in 1987 'to preserve and enhance' buildings

Fig 71 (opposite, top) *Interior of the cell block at Newton Street Police Station Museum [DP024959]*

Fig 72 (opposite, bottom) *The former site of 36 Back Turner Street. [DP028888]*

and their settings, often down to some of the smallest external details. Conservation area designation recognises that an area can be a complex entity, enshrining a powerful sense of the past, of continuity and of sense of place – even if many of the constituent buildings don't merit individual listing.

In addition to these legal controls and the best-practice advice contained in Planning Policy Guidelines, English Heritage, through its developing Area grant schemes, has already contributed over £500,000 to safeguard this fragile historic area, including grants to such important buildings as the Newton Street Police Station Museum (Fig 71). With the City Council it also jointly funded a Buildings at Risk Register to ensure that scarce resources are properly targeted at those highly graded buildings most in need, for there have been notable losses – especially early small-scale buildings such as 36 and 38 Back Turner Street, rare surviving links with the domestic industries of the 18th century, which collapsed catastrophically in 2005 (Fig 72). Many other structures are key buildings awaiting owners, developers and architects with the vision, determination and talent to find new uses for them.

By using the legal tools at our disposal and giving expert advice and grant aid, English Heritage seeks to save the best of the past and enhance its setting for present and future generations. It has been proved time and time again that the sensitive re-use and adaptation of our heritage forms the cornerstone of successful regeneration schemes. If the mistakes of the past are not to be repeated, it is vital that conservation of the historical environment be put at the heart of our thinking about development, for if the uniqueness of the Northern Quarter is not cherished, future generations will be unable to place themselves in a historical continuum, measure the present against the past, or feel a sense of identity and belonging. English Heritage believes firmly that everyone values "a sense of place" and that recognition of how an area has developed, what makes its special, and how an individual fits into that history can be life-enriching.

Manchester is now a leader in urban regeneration and finds itself faced with challenges which could alter it as readily – for good or ill – as at any time in its past. Fitting the new into the old is an essential part of this challenge, fuelling a continuing debate about the city's heritage that constantly renews and re-evaluates people's sense of self, and their wishes for their future environment. The Northern Quarter can become a key contributor to Manchester's future as the centre of a vibrant city region, but to succeed it must also open up and re-connect with the rest of the city and provide a vital physical link between Ancoats and Piccadilly Gardens, and between Piccadilly Basin and Victoria Station. It needs to become an area where niche retailers can benefit from new office workers, where residents can enjoy an oasis of city-centre calm whilst also benefiting from new services, and where people want to walk again. It must resist the urge to make a pastiche of itself and avoid becoming a heritage theme park devoid of good contemporary architecture, but it must also resist the worst excesses of corporate identity and global shop-fronts and search instead for an individual identity generated from its own powerful sense of place.

# Further reading

Goodall, I and Taylor, S 2001 The Shudehill and Northern Quarter of Manchester: 'An Outgrowth of Accident' and 'Built According to a Plan' *Architectural Investigation* Reports and Papers B/066/2001. Swindon: English Heritage.

Hartwell, Clare 2001 *Manchester*. London: Penguin Books.

Hylton, Stuart 2003 *A History of Manchester*. Chichester: Philimore.

Kidd, A 2002 *Manchester*, 3 edn. Edinburgh: Edinburgh University Press.

McDonald, Ian (ed) 2004 *Manchester: Shaping the City*. London: RIBA

Parkinson-Bailey, John J 2000 *Manchester: An Architectural History*. Manchester: Manchester University Press.

Taylor, S, Cooper, M and Barnwell, P S 2002 *Manchester: The Warehouse Legacy: An Introduction and Guide*. London: English Heritage.

Williams, Mike with Farnie, D A 1992 *Cotton Mills in Greater Manchester*. Preston: Carnegie Publishing Ltd.

# Other titles in the Informed Conservation series

*Behind the Veneer: The South Shoreditch furniture trade and its buildings.* Joanna Smith and Ray Rogers, 2006. Product code 51204, ISBN 9781873592960

*The Birmingham Jewellery Quarter: An introduction and guide.* John Cattell and Bob Hawkins, 2000. Product code 50205, ISBN 9781850747772

*Bridport and West Bay: The buildings of the flax and hemp industry.* Mike Williams, 2006. Product code 51167, ISBN 9781873592861

*Building a Better Society: Liverpool's historic institutional buildings.* Colum Giles, 2008. Product code 51332, ISBN 9781873592908

*Built on Commerce: Liverpool's central business district.* Joseph Sharples and John Stonard, 2008. Product code 51331, ISBN 9781905624348

*Built to Last? The buildings of the Northamptonshire boot and shoe industry.* Kathryn A Morrison with Ann Bond, 2004. Product code 50921, ISBN 9781873592793

*Gateshead: Architecture in a changing English urban landscape.* Simon Taylor and David Lovie, 2004. Product code 52000, ISBN 9781873592762

*Manchester: The warehouse legacy – An introduction and guide.* Simon Taylor, Malcolm Cooper and P S Barnwell, 2002. Product code 50668, ISBN 9781873592670

*Margate's Seaside Heritage.* Nigel Barker, Allan Brodie, Nick Dermott, Lucy Jessop and Gary Winter, 2007. Product code 51335, ISBN 9781905624669

*Newcastle's Grainger Town: An urban renaissance.* Fiona Cullen and David Lovie, 2003. Product code 50811, ISBN 9781873592779

*'One Great Workshop': The buildings of the Sheffield metal trades.* Nicola Wray, Bob Hawkins and Colum Giles, 2001. Product code 50214, ISBN 9781873592663

*Ordinary Landscapes, Special Places: Anfield, Breckfield and the growth of Liverpool's suburbs.* Adam Menuge, 2008. Product code 51343, ISBN 9781873592892

*Places of Health and Amusement: Liverpool's historic parks and gardens.* Katy Layton-Jones and Robert Lee, 2008. Product code 51333, ISBN 9781873592915

*Religion and Place in Leeds.* John Minnis with Trevor Mitchell, 2007. Product code 51337, ISBN 9781905624485

*Religion and Place: Liverpool's historic places of worship.* Sarah Brown and Peter de Figueiredo, 2008. Product code 51334, ISBN 9781873592885

*Storehouses of Empire: Liverpool's historic warehouses.* Colum Giles and Bob Hawkins, 2004. Product code 50920, ISBN 9781873592809

*Stourport-on-Severn: Pioneer town of the canal age.* Colum Giles, Keith Falconer, Barry Jones and Michael Taylor, 2007. Product code 51290, ISBN 9781905624362

*Weymouth's Seaside Heritage.* Allan Brodie, Colin Ellis, David Stuart and Gary Winter, 2008. Product code 51429, ISBN 9781848020085

£7.99 each (plus postage and packing)

To order
Tel: EH Sales  01761 452966
Email: ehsales@gillards.com

Online bookshop: www.english-heritage.org.uk

## Map of the Northern Quarter showing key buildings

1   47–53 Tib Street
2   36–38 Back Turner Street
3   1–5 Kelvin Street
4   47 Piccadilly
5   8 Lever Street
6   12–14 Lever Street
7   2 Union Street
8   39 Hilton Street
9   69–77 Lever Street
10  The City public house, Oldham Street
11  The Castle public house, Oldham Street
12  Taylor's thread-winding mill, Stevenson Square
13  Dale Warehouse, Dale Street
14  Jackson's Warehouse, Tariff Street
15  Smithfield Market Hall, Swan Street
16  Wholesale Fish Market, High Street
17  Retail Fish Market, Oak Street
18  Market Buildings, Thomas Street
19  Adelphi Hotel, Piccadilly
20  Brunswick Hotel, Piccadilly
21  Methodist Central Hall, Oldham Street
22  Wellington Inn, Back Piccadilly
23  48–50 Thomas Street and 7 Kelvin Street
24  49 Piccadilly
25  33 Dale Street, Bradley House
26  18–20 Hilton Street
27  75–77 High Street
28  7 Dale Street
29  16–18 Tariff Street, Fourways House
30  64–66 Dale Street
31  Eleska House, Dale Street
32  Langley Buildings, Dale Street
33  Industry House, Dale House
34  Pall Mall House, 'The Coliseum', Church Street
35  Rylands Building, Market Street
36  31–35 Goadsby Street

37  1–11 Newton Street
38  55–61 Piccadilly
39  1 Piccadilly
40  77–83 Piccadilly
41  69–75 Piccadilly
42  Henry Jacob, 87 Oldham Street
43  26 Oldham Street
44  28–40 Oldham Street
45  46–48 Copperas Street
46  Lower Turk's Head public house, Shudehill
47  Hare and Hounds public house, Shudehill
48  Stovells Buildings, Shudehill
49  60a Oldham street: 'Lennard's'
50  76–80 Oldham Street: 'Dobbins'
51  21–31 Oldham Street
52  6–12 Oldham Street
53  46–50 Oldham Street: 'Marks & Spencer'
54  101–103 Oldham Street: 'Burton's'
55  19–21 Piccadilly: 'Woolworths'
56  13–19 Oldham Street: 'C&A Modes'
57  135–141 Oldham Street: 'Cantors', latterly the offices of *The Big Issue in the North*
58  24–32 High Street
59  Bishopsgate House, Great Ancoats Street
60  Chatsworth House, Lever Street
61  Hilton House, Hilton Street
62  Arndale Centre
63  Affleck's Palace, Church Street
64  38–40 Hilton Street
65  Smithfield Building, Oldham Street
66  Pink One, Thomas Street
67  Newton Buildings, Newton Street
68  Burton Building, Oldham Street
69  7–9 Swan Street
70  Newton Street Police Station Museum

Back cover
*Faraday Street entrance to A. Division Police Station, now the Greater Manchester Police Museum and entered from Newton Street.*
*[DP028444]*